LITTLE CRAFT BOOK SERIES

MACRAMÉ

By Imelda Manalo Pesch

Photographs by John Pesch

Creative Knotting
Braiding
Twisting

Threads
Cords
Yarns

STERLING PUBLISHING CO., INC. NEW YORK

Oak Tree Press Co., Ltd.
Distributed by WARD LOCK, Ltd., London & Sydney

SAUNDERS OF TORONTO, Ltd., Don Mills, Canada

Little Craft Book Series

Candle-Making
Corrugated Carton Crafting
Creating with Beads
Creating with Burlap
Coloring Papers
Felt Crafting
Macramé
Making Paper Flowers
Metal and Wire Sculpture
Model Boat Building
Nail Sculpture
Potato Printing
Repoussage
Scissorscraft
Whittling and Wood Carving

419 Park Avenue South, New York, N.Y. 10016

British edition published by Oak Tree Press Co., Ltd.
Distributed in Great Britain and the Commonwealth by
Ward Lock, Ltd., 116 Baker Street, London W1
Manufactured in the United States of America

Library of Congress Catalog Card No.: 76–126848
ISBN 0–8069–5158–3 U.K. 7061 2261 5
5159–1

Contents

Before You Begin

Macramé, a technique of knotting using cords or suitable yarns, is creative work. This book will show you how fascinating this simple craft is and how you can produce very charming pieces for both functional and ornamental purposes. The projects shown here may look complicated to you at first, but you will soon find that they are really very simple, once you have mastered a few basic knots. And you have been tying knots daily without even being conscious of it!

Macramé has gained an increasing popularity in the last few years as a revival from the past. Originally practiced in southern Europe between the 14th and 16th centuries, it is now adapted to modern fashion and décor. Items made by this technique are remarkably strong as well as beautiful. You are bound to project your hidden artistic talent when you create in this medium. This craft deserves its place in many museums all over the world. A knowledge of macramé is indeed well worth acquiring.

Before you begin, you will need some pointers to guide you. You do not need any special instruments—only your own two hands. You will control the tightness of the knots and even of the design itself.

Hold the cords in any way that is convenient for you. As you work along, you will discover how you prefer to manipulate the materials.

Work the knots slightly tighter when making projects that will be subjected to much stress than when making those that are intended to hang or lay flat.

Either a table top or your lap may serve as a working area. You will, however, need a *Working Base* (WB) on which to anchor your work, to keep it secure while you pull the cords or tighten the knots. A firm polyurethane foam pillow is ideal for this purpose. The upholstered arm or back of a chair, nails on a wood board or even a door knob or hook on the wall will do as well.

You will also need a few simple aids, such as *plastic-* or *glass-head pins* to fasten the cords onto the WB. Use them liberally so that your work is anchored securely. A *ruler* or *tape-measure* and a pair of *scissors* will be needed for measuring and cutting the cords. Other accessories which may be helpful will be mentioned later.

Materials

A multitude of *cords* or *twines*—cotton, nylon, jute, plastic, linen or sisal—are easily found at the packaging departments of grocery, hardware and variety stores, and marine or upholstery supply stores. *Rug yarns*—wool, cotton or rayon—can be found at knitting and crocheting shops or weaving and rug-hooking supply stores.

Use materials which are firmly twisted or evenly well-rounded with good body, preferably without thick and thin parts. The cord should be strong enough to survive the tension applied while working the knots. Slippery, elastic, or soft yarns do not give satisfactory results. Each project demands a certain type of material, depending upon the purpose of the article.

Illus. 1. Tools and aids for macramé: Macramé Working Base (WB) (a small polyurethane pillow, attached to a piece of wood board), cords and rug yarn, head pins, ruler, scissors, C-clamps, crochet hook and rubber bands.

Basic Knots

Now, let us make a decorative piece (Illus. 7) using one kind of basic knot, the DOUBLE KNOT (DK). Most knotters enjoy this knot because of the variety of designs one can create with it. First, you must learn to make a BEAD KNOT. Take any packaging cord you might have around your house. Now, measure and cut four pieces, each 80 inches long.

Naturally, the length of the cords you cut will determine the length of the finished project. If you are a beginner in the art of macramé, you might want to allow more than 80 inches for each piece in this first project, as you might knot more loosely than average and would therefore require more cord. Until you know your personal requirements, allow some leeway when you measure and cut.

Bead Knot

Mounting of cords: Cut another piece of cord about 10 inches long, and make a BEAD KNOT (BK) (directions for making this knot appear below) near the left end and another BK near the right end (Illus. 2).

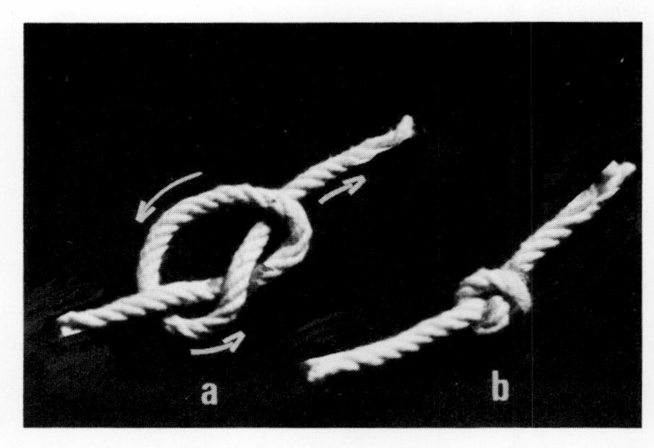

Illus. 2. Bead Knot (BK). a: Arrows show how end is twisted around and drawn through. b: Completed BK.

A Bead Knot is made by bringing one (or more) strand of cord around itself, then drawing the end through the space made. In *a*, arrows show how the end is drawn through, then tightened. A completed BK is shown in *b*.

Fasten each BK with a head pin onto the WB so that the 10-inch cord lies horizontally. We shall call this cord the *Foundation Knot Bearer* (Fnd.KB). Take one 80-inch strand and fold it in half. Notice that a *loop* is made at one end, and each cord now will measure 40 inches.

Following Illus. 3*a*, place the loop under the Fnd.KB; *b*: fold (opened) forward over the Fnd. KB and the two cords; *c*: take these two cords through the loop; *d*: pull tight and let the ends hang downward.

Repeat this procedure with the other long strands. Fasten all mounted loops securely with head pins. When working with extra long strands, this mounting may be simplified. First fold the open loop backward and bring the two "lobes" together. Then slip onto the Fnd.KB and pull tightly into place. Some knotters prefer to use the underside view of this mounting as shown in Illus. 3*e*. Whatever you prefer, it is always wise to be consistent. Let us call this mounting *Method A*, for reference. We will discuss some other methods as we go along.

We will number the cords from left to right: 1, 2, 3, 4, 5, 6, 7 and 8. See Illus. 6*a*. Take #1 and lay over all the cords horizontally towards the right.

We shall call #1 the *Knot Bearer* (KB), defined as the cord which carries the knots or around which the knot is made; #2, 3, 4, 5, 6, 7 and 8 the *Working Threads* (WT), defined as the cord which is twisted around the KB to make the knot. Make 7 successive DOUBLE KNOTS (directions for making this knot is shown in Illus. 4), using #1 as KB and each of #2 to #8 as WT's.

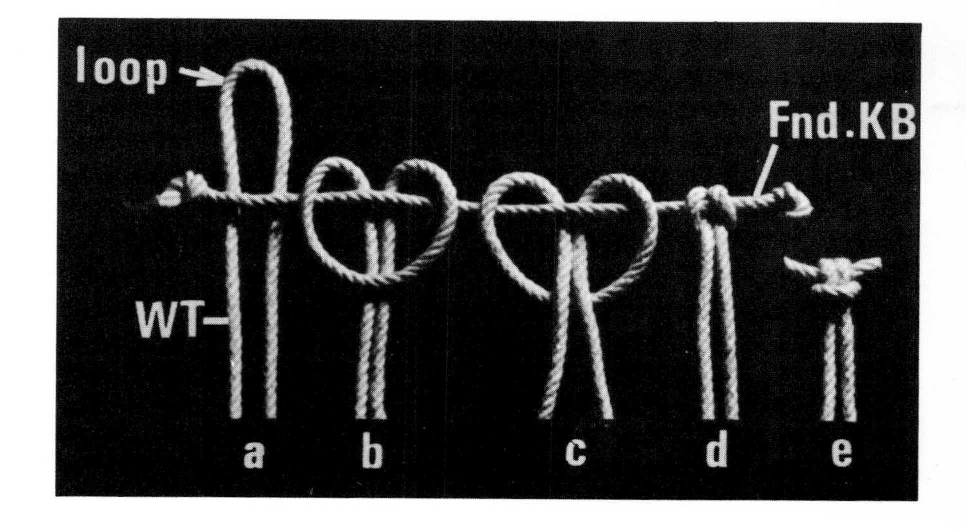

Illus. 3. Mounting Method A.

Double Knot

This knot consists of a KB and a WT. It is made by passing the WT from under the KB around (towards the left); the first twist is shown in *a*. This is then repeated, so that it passes and is caught between the two twists. The second twist is

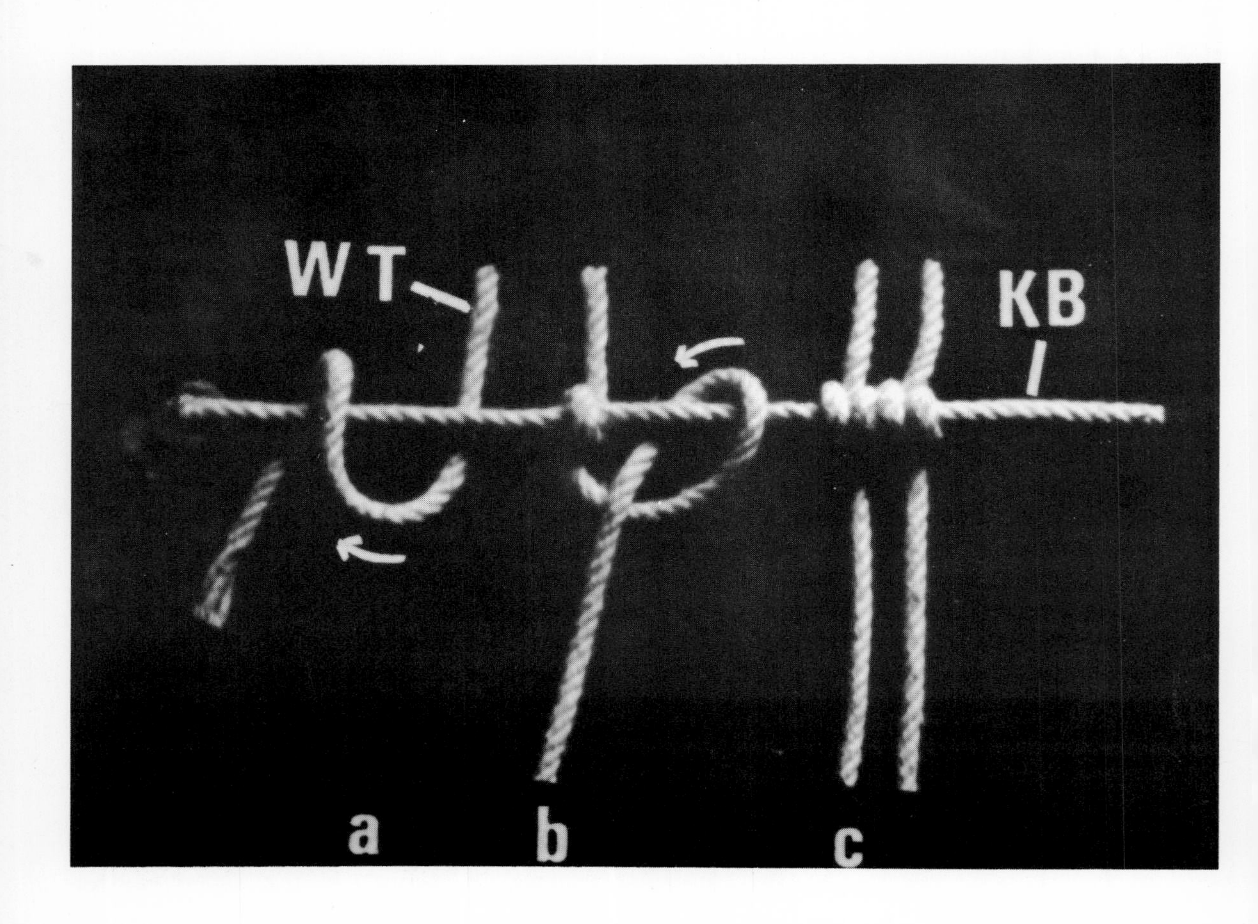

Illus. 4. How to tie a Double Knot (DK).

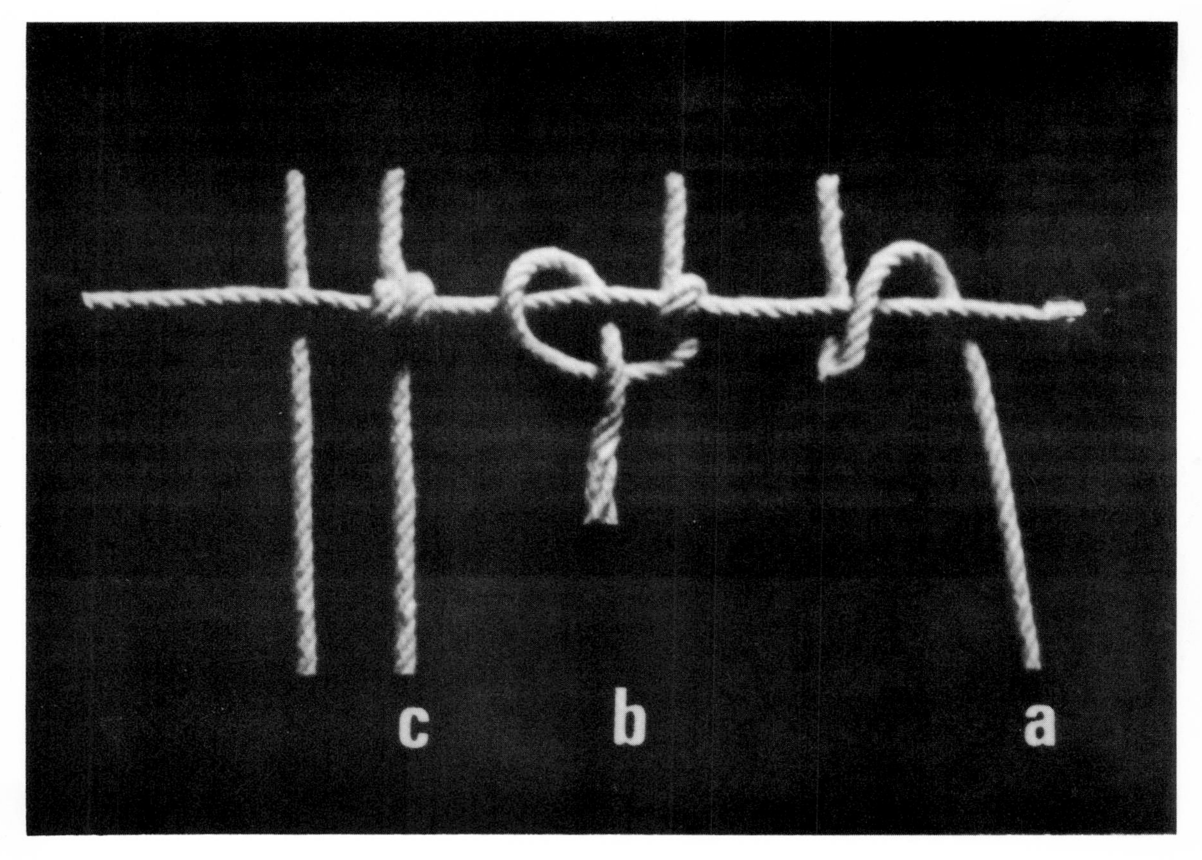

Illus. 5. Reverse of DK in Illus. 4.

pictured in *b*. Pull the end of the cord tightly downward. REMEMBER: Hold the KB taut at all times while twisting the WT. This knot may be made towards either the left or the right direction. When progressing towards the right direction, the KB is held by the right hand, and the WT is twisted by the left hand. When progressing towards the left direction, the KB is held by the left hand and the WT is twisted by the right hand. Illus. 5 shows the reverse of Illus. 4. As you have seen, you may use one or more WT's with one KB.

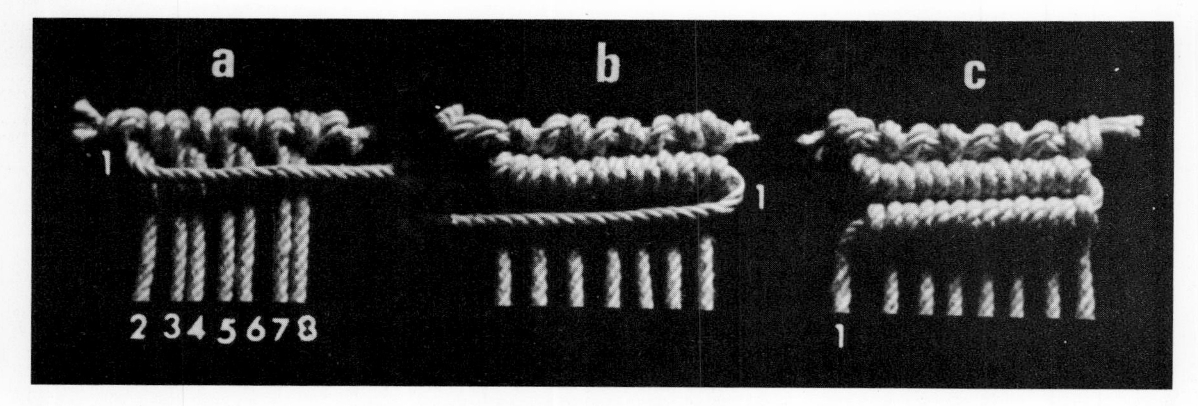

Illus. 6A. Formation of Horizontal DK bars.

After making 7 successive DK's, you have made a *Horizontal DK bar* (Hor.DK bar), as in Illus. 6*b*. Reverse this bar to make a second Hor. DK bar, using the same KB (Illus. 6*c*).

Design: Series I: Divide the cords into two groups of four. Taking #1 as KB, lay it diagonally over the next three cords towards the right, and then make three successive DK's in the order of #2, 3 and 4. You have now made a *Right Diagonal DK bar* (R Diag.DK bar) as shown in Illus. 6*d*. Reverse this with the second group (right half); i.e., take #8 as KB and lay it across the other three cords diagonally (at the same angle) and make three successive DK's in the order of #7, 6 and 5. Using the same KB (#8), make a DK in the same direction (left) with the

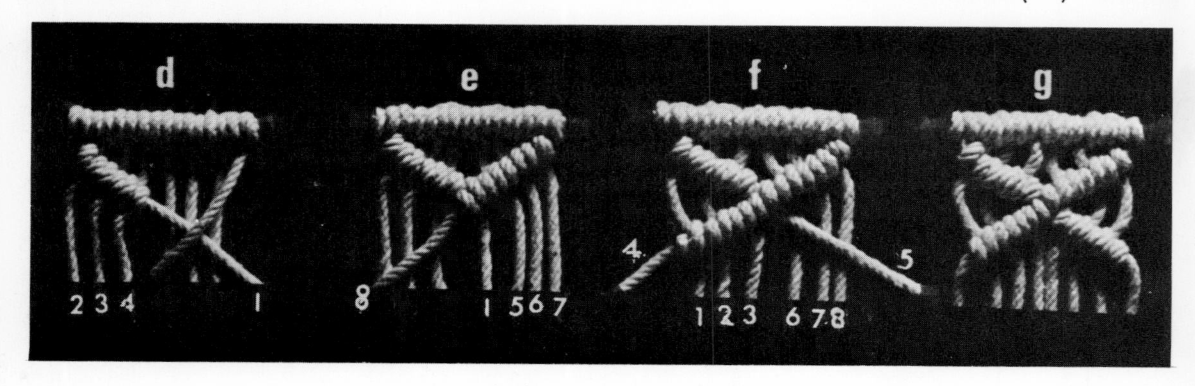

Illus. 6B. Formation of Diagonal DK bars.

left KB (#1). You have now made a *Left Diagonal DK bar* (L Diag.DK bar), joined to the R Diag. DK bar in the middle by another DK, Illus. 6*e*.

Series II: Using the same KB (#8), which is now the fourth cord, continue to make a L Diag. DK bar with #3, 2 and 1 (Illus. 6*f*).

Series III: Using the fifth cord as KB (the same KB used in Series I: #1), continue to make a R Diag.DK bar with #6, 7 and 8. Fasten each end of the diagonal bars with head pins (Illus. 6*g*).

Repeat the design (Series I to Series III) until you have completed eight "X"s.

Finishing: With #1 as KB make 2 Hor.DK bars the same way you did at the start. Then cut the cord ends evenly about 1-inch long.

This piece may be worked out into a longer piece as an arm or legband, curtain tieback, or still longer, as a head or waistband. Cutting cords for longer lengths is discussed under the section titled Measuring and Cutting Strands, page 21.

You may even start to knot a piece of macramé with the intent of making one certain item, but change your mind along the way and decide to use the piece for something else instead. One of the wonderful aspects of macramé is that you are free to change your mind, free to add new patterns in the middle of a design, and free to use the piece as you wish. Even a finished article is suitable for many different uses: a belt, neckpiece or head-band from one pattern, or a place mat, wall hanging or rug from another.

Illus. 7. Band using Double Knots.

Review of Instructions

As you have seen, cords frequently change places or cross each other during the knotting. It is therefore necessary to divide the instructions for a design into "Series" (Ser.) in order to avoid confusion in numbering the cords. Thus we number the cords from left to right: #1, 2, 3, etc., within the group of cords in each Series. Then they are numbered from Series to Series. That means that cords are numbered in Series II from #1 to 8, *regardless* of the numbering in Series I. Likewise, cords in Series III are numbered from #1 to 8, regardless of the numbering in Series II.

Occasionally a Series is composed of more than one step. It is then further divided into "Sub-Series." Sometimes a project contains "Rows" of designs.

It is advisable to complete one Series of knots across the whole width of the work before proceeding to the next Series, when the design is repeated. The knots are more even and it also eliminates possibly omitting some cords along the line. However, some knotters are eager to see the completed design at once before proceeding to the next Series. In this case, you may work at least three or even four groups at a time, but be sure to leave the right half of the last working group free for the next group.

In the case of long fringes, loops may be added on in mounting, little by little as the work progresses. Where the width of your project is only

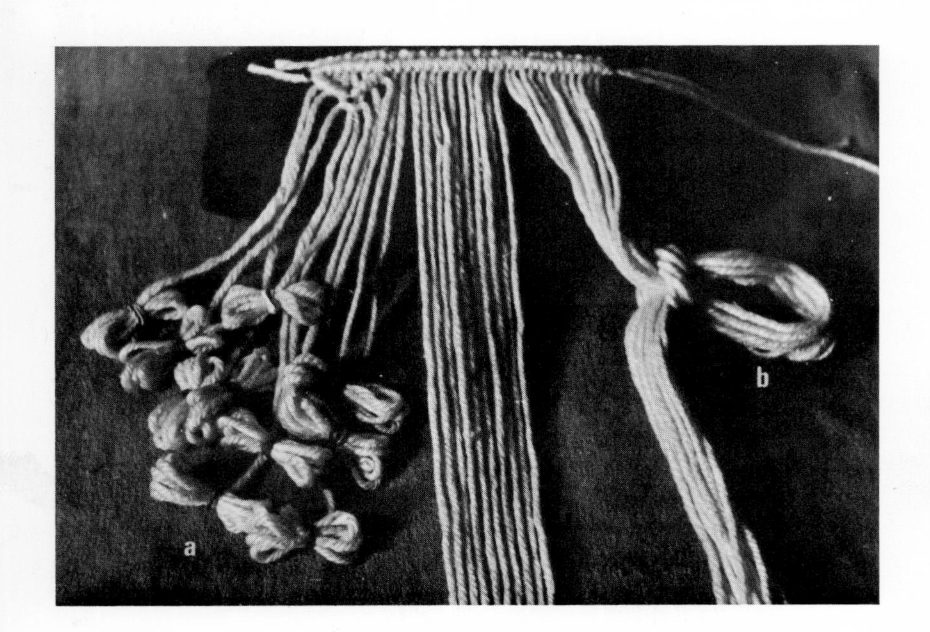

Illus. 8. a: Rubber bands used to shorten strands temporarily. b: How to bundle a section of the Working Threads (WT).

Illus. 9. Fringe using Double Knots.

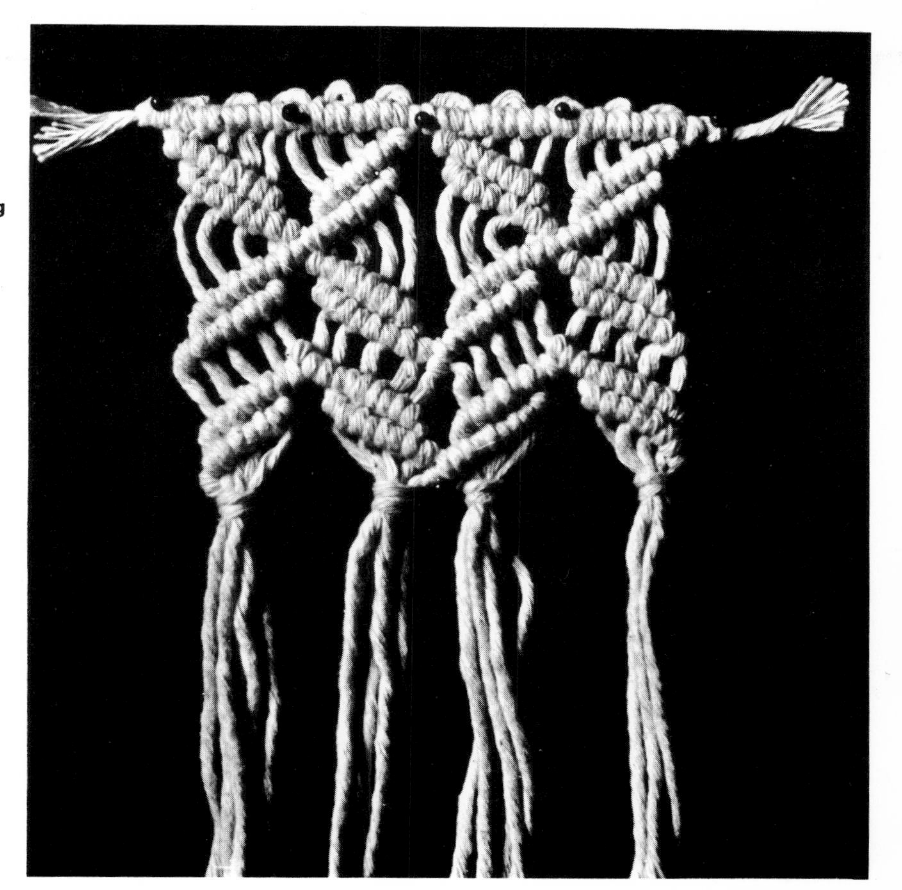

one or a few feet, such as with a handbag, place mat or wall hanging, you may bundle strands into sections so that this part is out of your way, while working on one section. See Illus. 8.

Now, let us make a fringe where the design is repeated across the width. Fringes can be used to trim many objects such as curtains, window shades, vanities, scarves, garments, bedspreads or anything you wish, to add a unique and personal design.

A Fringe Using DK's (Illus. 9)

Recommended material: heavy, dyed cotton cord or rug yarn. Measure and cut 10 strands, each 32 inches long.

Illus. 10. a: Mounted loop on fabric edge. b: Insert loop from underside of fabric edge with the aid of crochet hook.

Mounting: If you intend to use this fringe for edging a scarf or any garment, you may mount directly onto the fabric edge in the same manner as for the above band, Method A. Use a *crochet hook* to insert the loop through the fabric edge from the underside (Illus. 10).

Otherwise, use the following method, *Method B* (Horizontal DK bar with picots): Take a Fnd. KB long enough to go across the width and secure it onto the WB as before. Fold the strands to form loops as in Method A. Fasten each loop (one at a time) behind the Fnd.KB and proceed to make a DK bar with each of the cords as WT's, leaving a small picot, or loop of yarn, above. See Illus. 9. This design is composed of 10 cords, divided into two groups of 5. It is made up of Double DK bars instead of Single DK bars, with "closed" ends (discussed in Design and Color, page 22). Number the cords: #1, 2, 3, 4, 5, 6, 7, 8, 9 and 10.

Design: Series I: R Diag.DK bar, using #1 as KB with #2, 3, 4 and 5 as WT's; then #2 as KB (now the first cord on the left) with #3, 4, 5 and 1 as WT's (Illus. 11*a* and 11*b*). You have just made "Closed Double" R Diag.DK bars.

Now, reverse on the right half: starting with #10 as KB, Closed Double L Diag.DK bars with #9 to 6 as WT's. Join the two groups at the center with another DK (same manner as in the above band).

Series II: Continue making Closed Double Diag.DK bars to make an "X" motif. Complete other designs across width. Join designs the same way as joining the halves of each design, with a DK.

Series III: About $\frac{1}{2}$ inch away from the preceding bars, R Diag.DK using #5 as KB and #6 as WT.

Series IV: Proceed to make another Closed Double L and then R Diag.DK bars, the same way as in the lower half of the preceding "X" motif. Complete across width, joining groups by a DK.

Finishing: Make tassels in groups of 5 cords, using two COLLECTING KNOTS.

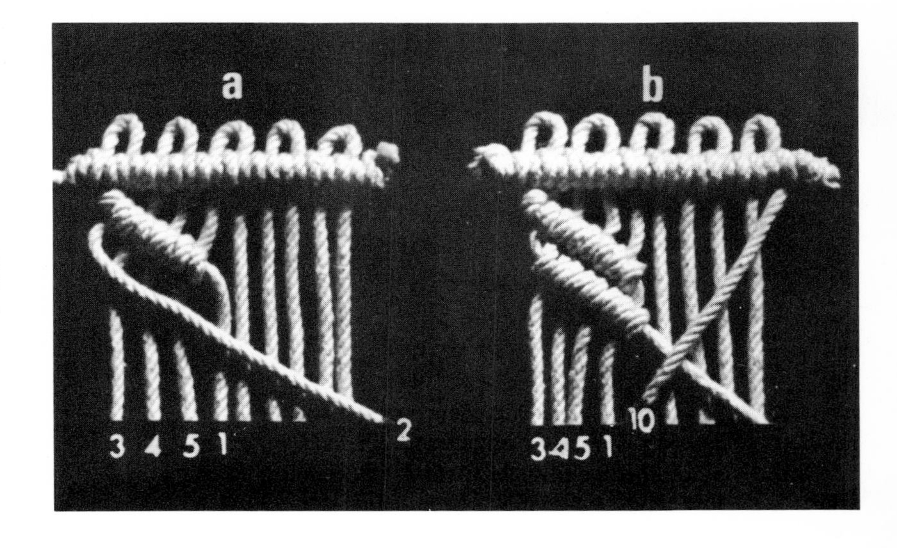

Illus. 11. Mounting Method B and formation of Closed Double R Diag. DK bars.

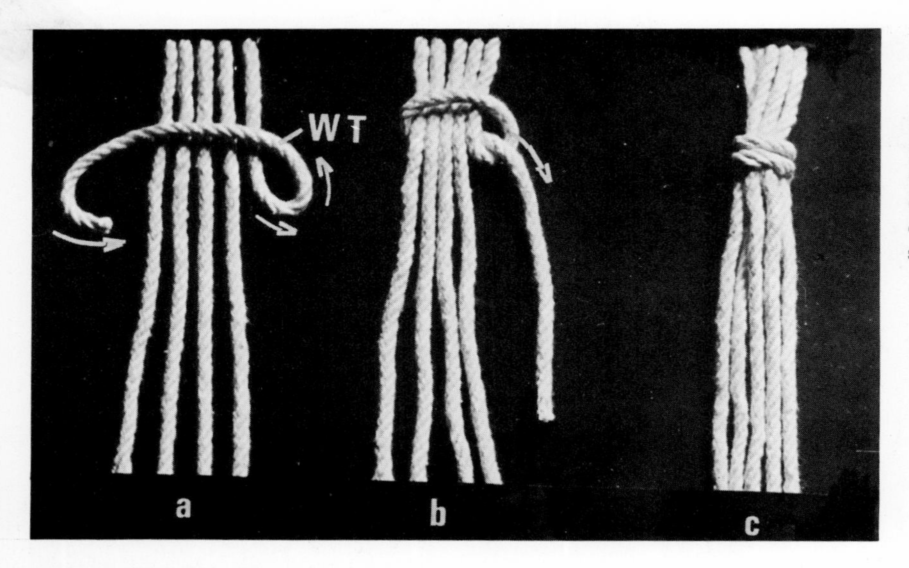

Illus. 12. Collecting Knot (CK). a: WT is twisted over, around, and b: drawn through space. c: 2 CK's used to make a secure knot for tassel.

Collecting Knots (CK) (Illus. 12)

A Collecting Knot is made by using a long cord as the WT to tie a group of cords together. Twist the long cord over and around, and draw it through the space made. Pull tightly and then repeat to make a more secure knot.

Cut cord ends evenly to the desired length. This fringe is sewn onto the edge of the article you intend to trim by using a needle and thread, or it may be pasted on.

Square Knot (Illus. 13)

Another basic macramé knot is the FLAT KNOT (FK). However, first you will have to learn how to tie a SIMPLE or SQUARE KNOT (SK). This is made by interlacing two cords.

a: Bend the left cord towards the right, and lay the right cord over this straight downward;

b–c: then bring it under the left cord and draw it out to make the first twist or crossing;

d–e: now, reverse: bend the right cord towards the left this time, and lay the left cord over and cross as above;

f: pull both ends tight with equal tension. The SK is completed.

Flat Knot (Illus. 14)

A Flat Knot is merely a SK with two middle cords caught in-between the crossings. It is made up of four cords: two outer WT's and two filler cords, which are the middle cords. The cords are numbered: #1, 2, 3 and 4, from left to right.

a: Bend #1 over #2 and 3; lay #4 over #1 straight downward.

Illus. 13. How to tie a Simple or Square Knot (SK).

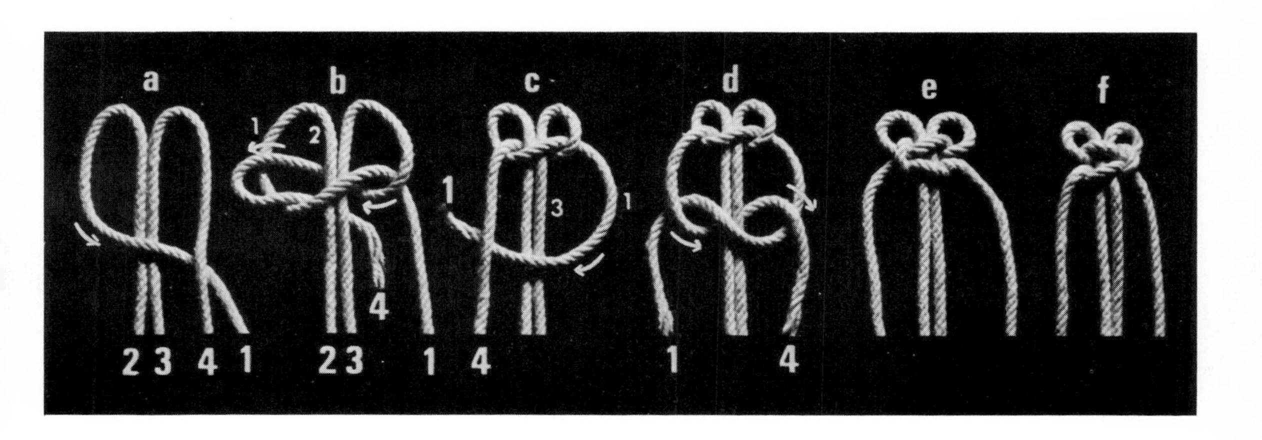

Illus. 14. How to tie a Flat Knot (FK).

b: Bring #4 under #1, then under #2 and 3 and draw out through the left space, between #1 and 2.

c: Pull both ends with equal tension, to bring the crossing into position. Reverse the first step by bending the right cord #1 over #2 and 3; lay #4 over #1 straight downward.

d: Bring #4 under #1, then under #2 and 3 and draw out through space between #3 and 1 (right hole).

e: Pull ends so that the second crossing lies next to the first crossing. The Flat Knot is completed.

You may catch #2 and 3 between your third and fourth fingers while pulling the cord ends. Some knotters prefer to use the reverse steps as

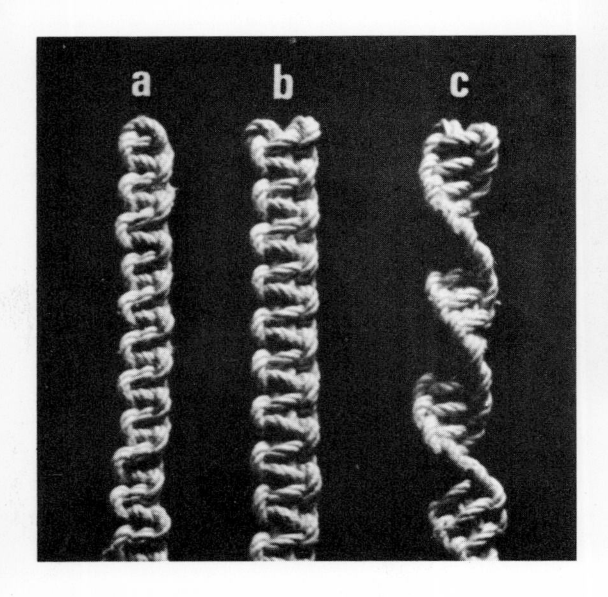

Illus. 15. Sinnets. a: SK sinnet. b: FK sinnet. c: Half FK sinnet.

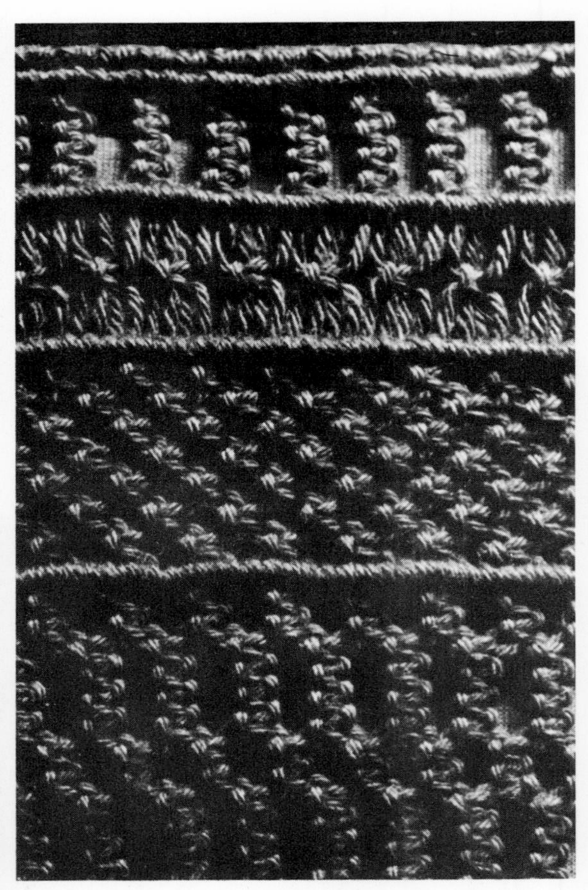

Illus. 16. 4 FK sinnets. Single FK's. Single FK's. 2 FK's and 4 FK sinnets.

Illus. 17. FK's with spaces in between. Single FK's. Double FK's.

shown in Illus. 14*f*. Whatever you prefer, be consistent.

Successive SK's or FK's form a band or a "sinnet" of SK's or FK's. (Illus. 15*a* and 15*b*). A sinnet of the first half of the SK (*Half SK*) or the first half of the FK (*Half FK*) (Illus. 15*c*) is also possible. Notice that this band automatically twists itself as the knots are made. When making the FK or Half FK sinnets, only the WT's (outer cords) go into the knot itself while the middle cords are just filler cords. Therefore, you will have to allow much longer lengths for these outer cords.

For convenience, you may tie the middle cords on a string tied around your waist, to hold them steadily while the knots are being made. FK's may be used to make a network or open-mesh design, as singles, doubles or multiples (Illus. 16). They may be set close to each other or far apart with spaces between the knots. (Illus. 17).

A FK with more than two filler cords in the middle is called a COLLECTING FLAT KNOT (CFK), as shown at the start of the band (Illus. 18).

A Band Using FK's (Illus. 18)

Recommended material: metallic or dyed cotton cord. This band is made up of FK's and CFK's.

Length of strands: Use six times (or three times, doubled) the length of the finished band for five strands, and eight times (or four times, doubled) the length of the finished band for one strand to be used as the outer WT's in the CFK's.

Mounting: Secure loops by tying them together with a piece of cord and fastening onto the WB with head pins. Allow about 3 inches for tassels: take one strand and make 3 or 4 CK's around all the cords. Using the two longer cords as WT's, make as many CFK's as you will need to make about 12 inches for tying with the other end of the band.

Divide into two groups of 6 cords and make two separate 4 CFK's sinnets.

Design: Diamond-shape network made up of FK's.

Series I: 3 FK's: (#1 to 4), (#5 to 8) and (#9 to 12).

Series II: 2 FK's: (#3 to 6) and (#7 to 10).

Series III: FK (#5 to 8).

Allow a space about $1\frac{1}{2}$ inches away from the last preceding FK and then reverse above steps—

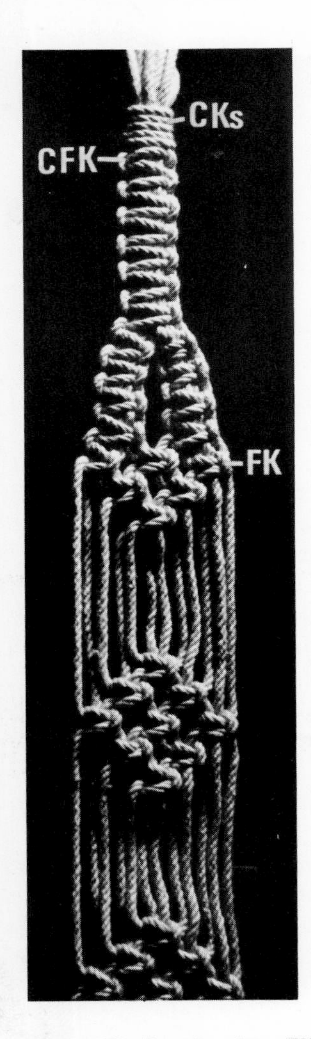

Illus. 18. Band using FK's and Collecting Flat Knots (CFK's).

beginning with Ser. III, Ser. II and Ser. I. Then repeat Ser. II and Ser. I to complete a diamond motif. Repeat the diamond motifs, allowing equal spaces in between, until the required length is completed.

Finishing: Reverse steps before Ser. I.

Button Hole Knot (BHK) (Illus. 19)

This knot is made up of the KB and WT also. To make a BHK:

a: Bring the WT over, around and out through the space between the two cords.

b: Reverse, this time by bringing under, around and out through the space between the two cords.

c: Pull the WT tight so that the two hitches lie close to each other.

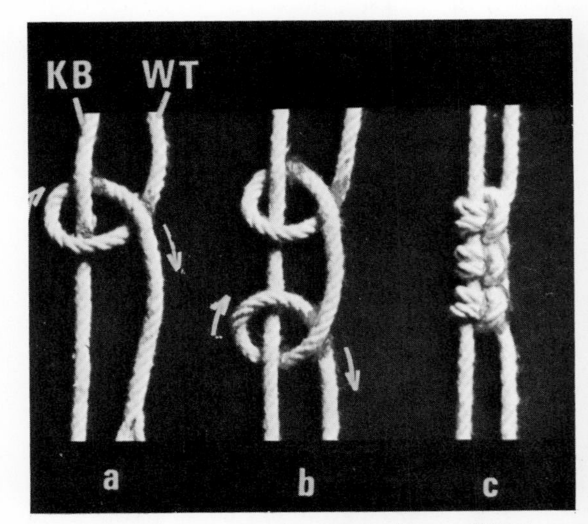

Illus. 19. Double Button Hole Knot (BHK). a: First twist (WT over KB). b: Second twist (WT under KB). c: 3 completed Button Hole Knots.

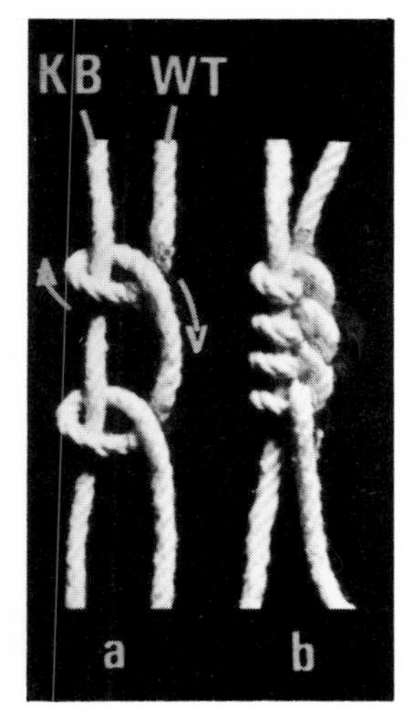

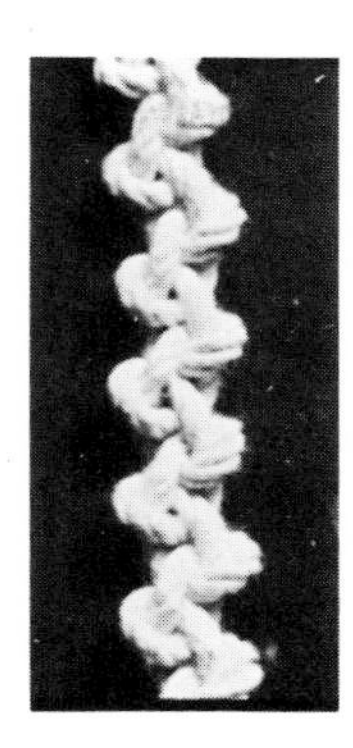

Illus. 20. a: How the WT is twisted around (over) the KB. b: 4 Single Button Hole Knots completed.

Illus. 21 (right). Chain of Single Button Hole Knots.

This is called a *Double Button Hole Knot* (Double BHK). It may be repeated into a band of Double BHK's. The first half of the Double BHK is called *Single BHK*, Illus. 20. A "*chain*" of Single BHK or Double BHK is made by alternating the KB with the WT. Illus. 21 shows a chain of Single BHK's.

Measuring and Cutting Strands

You have noticed that in mounting, each strand is folded into half its length, before you actually mount the cords or loops. We therefore find it easier to measure the cords to the required length and then double them. You will then handle shorter lengths. All lengths for mounting suggested in the following projects are thus doubled. A pair of *C-clamps* set apart at a correct distance on a table top is very convenient. Tie one end of the cord to a C-clamp, and wind around between the two C-clamps as many times as the required number of strands. Then cut all cords at one time with a pair of scissors at the starting point. Your cords will automatically be doubled, with loops produced at the other end. As you have already seen, loops are mounted before you can actually begin to tie the knots themselves. You might also use two chairs, two nails or two doorknobs at the correct distance apart. For shorter lengths, as for fringes, a piece of hard cardboard the right length will do.

When working with extra long strands, such as for waistbands, rubber bands may be used to shorten cords temporarily (Illus. 8). Wind each cord, starting from its end, around your four fingers, then wind a rubber band at the middle to hold them in place. You can easily let out more lengths as needed. Otherwise, you may just let them hang straight down to the floor. Usually only one cord is pulled at a time while making the knots, so that tangling seldom occurs.

When working on bigger projects such as pillow-tops, handbags, window shades, room dividers or wall hangings, it is advisable to work a sample about 3 inches square, using the design and cord you intend to use in your project. The density of the knots that go into the design affects the length of your cords. Where the design uses few knots, you will need only about three times the total length (doubled, of course), and where the design takes up more knots, you will need as much as 5, 6 or more times (doubled) with a very dense design. A heavier cord usually takes up more length than a lighter one using the same design.

The length of the cord used up in the sample piece is equal to the initial length minus the length of the leftover cord. The resulting figure divided by 3 (inches) would be the amount used up per inch of the work. Multiply this by the total length of the finished project, doubling the length for each strand folded into two cords. The number of strands per inch across the width, multiplied by the total width of the finished project, will determine the total number of strands you will need.

For example, suppose you are using 16-inch strands (doubled) to make a sample piece. When you finish, there is a piece left over of 4 inches. You have used 12 inches to make the 3-inch sample. Thus 12 divided by 3 equals 4. You will, therefore, need 4 times (doubled) the total length of the finished project. If you wish to make a 10-inch bag, you will need at least 40-inch (doubled) strands. If you used 4 strands per inch across the width, you will then need 4 times 10 or 40 strands to make a 10-inch wide bag.

It is also wise to be generous and not to stretch the strands while measuring. If, however, you find later that the lengths allowed are still too short, you may add a new strand. Firmly knot the required piece by SK or BK and then tack the unsightly ends on the underside of the work by inserting the cord ends through the loops of adjacent knots with the aid of a crochet hook.

Design and Color

Designs are made by combining one or more kinds of knots. The projects we have discussed so far are made of one kind of basic knot, DK's or FK's. Other projects will be made of combinations of different kinds of knots. There is no limit to the variety of combinations or patterns your imagination can create. This book can only show you a few of the possible designs, with the hope that you will be able to create your own after trying some of the projects shown here.

DK bars may be made horizontally, vertically, diagonally or curved. In the first and second

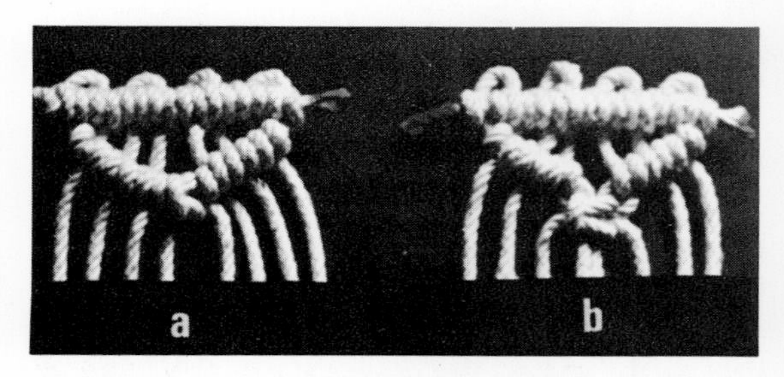

Illus. 22. a: Joining bars by SK. b: Joining bars by FK.

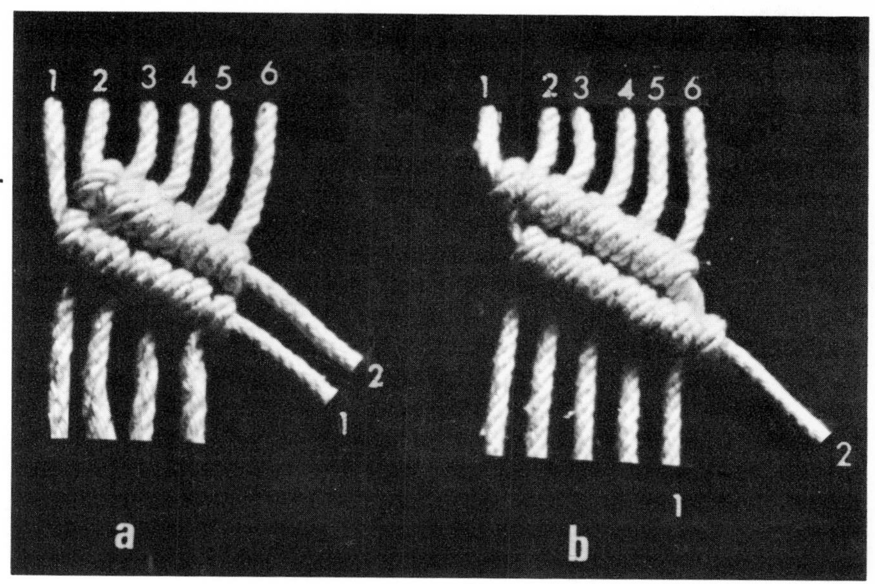

Illus. 23. a: "Open" bars. b: "Closed" bars.

pieces shown earlier, the left and right diagonal bars were joined by another DK. They may also be joined by SK (Illus. 22*a*) or FK (Illus. 22*b*).

One DK bar may be made to lie close to another DK bar, or set apart with spaces between them, as in the fringe in Illus. 9. Double or multiple bars may be "open" or "closed" depending on how their ends are finished off.

In Illus. 23*a*, cord #2 is first used as the KB and #3 to 6 as the WT's; then in the second bar, #1 is used as KB and #3 to 6 as the WT's, leaving both ends of the bars "open." Thus it is called "*Open Double R Diag.DK bars.*" In *b*, #1 is first used as the KB and #2 to 6 as the WT's; then in the second bar #2 is used as the KB and #3 to 6 and #1 as WT's, thereby closing the end of the first bar. Thus, it is called "*Closed Double R Diag.DK bars.*" This is also shown in the fringe in Illus. 9.

Motifs may be repeated across the width or down the length of the work. One may be alternated with another motif or motifs. Again, there is no rule. The more freedom you use in designing, the more interesting your results will be. Illus. 47 shows a piece where there is no definite pattern or motif. The designs in this book are only a few of the possible combinations which may serve as your guide to creating your own pieces.

Color plays an important role in designing. Different color effects may be achieved because the cords often change places. As you have noticed, in a DK, the KB is concealed by the WT, so that the color of the WT is what appears on the face. In Illus. 25, only one design was used in all three pieces, yet the positions or quantities of each color strand are different from each other. A new strand of a different color may be introduced at any point. In the bag shown in Illus. 31, a second color was introduced by using gold cords as WT's attached by DK's. Mosaic patterns are made by interchanging the WT's with the KB's.

Making Designs

Band in Illus. 24

Recommended material: Dyed cotton cord.

Length of strands: 7 times (doubled) the length of the finished band.

Mounting: Use two curtain rings (1 inch in diameter) or make rings by tying ends of a 5-inch strand into a SK. Use one ring as the Fnd.KB and mount 5 loops by Method A. Take last cord on the right and cover the rest of the ring with Double BHK's. Tack its end on the underside of the mounted loops.

Design: Series I: 2 FK's (#1 to 4); FK (#5 to 8).

Series II: Closed Double L Diag.DK bars, starting with #9 as KB and #8 to 1 as WT's.

Series III: 2 FK's (#2 to 5); 4 FK's (#6 to 9).

Series IV: Reverse Ser. II.

Continue to make FK's and Double bars in a zigzag pattern.

Finishing: Finish off by reversing steps before Ser. I. (Tie cord ends onto the second ring on the

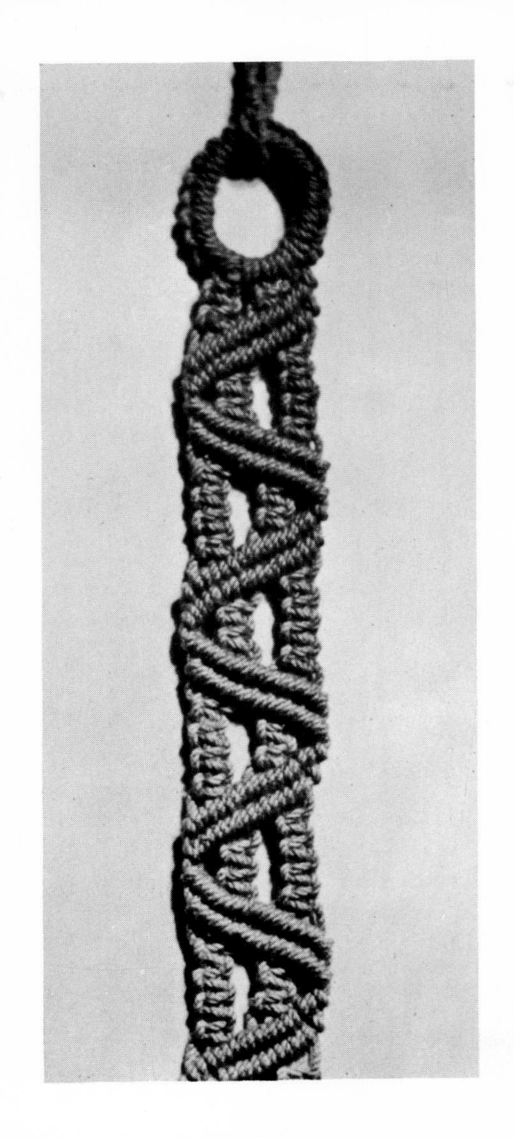

Illus. 24. Band made with dyed heavy cotton cord.

Illus. 25. Only one design was used to make these three pieces. Different effects were obtained by changing the proportions and positions of the colored threads.

underside.) Use a simple braid to tie two rings together.

Design in Illus. 25

Mount loops by Method A or Method B.

Design is composed of 12 cords (#1 to 12) and is repeated across the work.

Series I: FK (#5 to 8).

Series II: Closed Triple R Diag.DK bar, starting with #1 as KB and #2 to 6 as WT's. Reverse on the right half. Join bars by FK (#5 to 8).

Series III: 9 Single BHK's chain (#12 with #1 of next group).

Series IV: Same as Ser. I.

Series V: Reverse Ser. II.

Join #12 with #1 of next group by SK.

Band in Illus. 26a *(see page 28)*

Recommended material: Metallic, dyed cotton or nylon cord.

Length of strands: Use four cords: inner cords should be the same length of the finished band, and outer cords should be at least four times the length of inner cords.

Mounting: Fasten two loops together with a pin onto the WB and make 7 FK's sinnet, using the outer longer cords as WT's.

Design: Series I: 3 Double BHK's using #2 as KB and #1 as WT; reverse on the right half (3 Double BHK's using #3 as KB and #4 as WT).

Series II: 2 FK's (#1 to 4). Repeat twice about $\frac{1}{2}$ inch apart.

Series III: Same as Ser. I.

Series IV: 2 FK's (#1 to 4). Repeat once about ½ inch away.

Repeat from Ser. I and so on until the desired length is completed.

Finishing: Finish off with 7 FK's sinnet and SK using double strands. Make a tassel with 2 CK's and tip off each strands with a BK, At the mounting end, insert a double strand through the loops and make a tassel, the same way as the other end.

Gold Band in Illus. 26e *(see page 28)*

Recommended material: Metallic, dyed cotton or nylon cord.

Length of strands: 4 times (doubled) the length of the finished band.

Mounting: Mount 3 loops by Method B, but use cord #1 as Fnd.KB. Make a second Hor.DK bar using the same KB toward the left.

Design: Series I: 2 CFK's (#1 and 6 as WT's) 1 inch away from the last DK bar.

Series II: SK (#3 and 4) 1 inch away from the last CFK. Closed Double L Diag.DK bars, starting with #3 as KB and #2 and 1 as WT's. Reverse on the right half.

Series III: Make a "*bud*" ½ inch away from the preceding bars in the following steps:

Sub-Series 1: R Diag.DK bar (#3 as KB with #4, 5 and 6).

Sub-Series 2: L Diag.DK bar (#3 as KB with #2 and 1).

Sub-Series 3: R Diag.DK bar (#3 as KB with #4 and 5).

Sub-Series 4: L Diag.DK (#3 as KB with #2).

Now reverse:

Sub-Series 5: L Diag.DK (#5 as KB with #3 crossed over #4).

Sub-Series 6: R Diag.DK bar (#2 as KB with #3 and 4).

You have made an inner petal.

Sub-Series 7: L Diag.DK bar (#6 as KB with #5 and 4).

Sub-Series 8: R Diag.DK bar (#1 as KB with #2 and 3).

Push up DK's on each KB's so that the inner petal pops up.

Sub-Series 9: R Diag.DK (#3 as KB with #4).

You have made an outer petal thereby completing the "bud."

Series IV: Reverse Ser. II ending with SK (#3 and 4).

Repeat designs (Ser. I to Ser. IV) until the desired length is completed.

Finishing: Finish off in the same manner as the mounting end and make a tassel with 2 CK's.

At the mounting end, insert a 7-inch cord through the picots and tie together into a SK. Add 2 more 6-inch strands (insert over the SK) and make a tassel with 2 CK's. Tip off each cord end with a BK (both ends).

Red Band in Illus. 26c *(see page 28)*

Recommended material: Heavy rug yarn, metallic, dyed cotton or nylon cords.

Length of strands: 4 times (doubled) the length of the finished band, but allowing longer outer cords (#1 and 6).

Mounting: Fasten 3 loops (with longer cords on the outside) with pins onto the WB. 2 CK's around all cords and cut loops to make a tassel.

Design is similar to that of the preceding gold band.

Series I: Make as many CFK's (#1 and 6 as

WT's) as needed for tying ends of band together.

Series II: Same as Ser. II to Ser. IV of gold band. (Illus. 26*e*.)

Series III: Repeat Ser. II.

Series IV: 10 CFK's (#1 and 6 as WT's).

Repeat designs until the desired length of band is completed.

Finishing: Finish off by reversing steps at the mounting end. Cut cord ends evenly for tassel.

Blue-Gold Band in Illus. 26d *(see page 28)*

Recommended material: Heavy rug yarns or dyed cotton cords.

Length of strands: $4\frac{1}{2}$ times (doubled) the length of the finished band.

Mounting: Mount 4 loops in the order of: 1 blue, 2 gold, 1 blue, by Method B, with about 2-inch picots (to be cut into fringes later).

Design: This design is similar to that of the first project in Illus. 7.

Series I: FK (#3 to 6) (gold cords).

Series II: Closed Double L Diag.DK bars, starting with #4 as KB and #3, 2 and 1 as WT's. Reverse on the right half.

Series III: FK (#3 to 6) at center (blue cords).

Series IV: Reverse Ser. II.

Join bars by FK (#3 to 6).

Repeat designs (Ser. II to Ser. IV) until the desired length is completed.

Finishing: Finish off as with the mounting end. Tie each group of blue cords into a BK.

Green-Blue Band in Illus. 26b
(see page 28)

Recommended material: Heavy rug yarns or dyed cotton cords.

Length of strands: 4 times (doubled) for green cords and 6 times (doubled) for blue cords, the length of the finished band.

Mounting: Mount 6 loops by Method B in the order of: 1 blue, 4 green, 1 blue. Fasten blue loops about 2 inches away from mounting line. Use the first cord (blue) on the left as Fnd.KB, and the last cord on the right as KB for the second Hor.DK bar. Tie each double strand of blue cords above the DK bars into BK's and cut loops.

Design: Series I: 2 SK's (#1 and 2); FK (#5 to 8); 2 SK's (#11 and 12). Closed Double R Diag. DK bars, starting with #3 as KB and #4, 5 and 6 as WT's. Reverse on the right half. Join DK bars by FK at center.

Series II: 4 Open L Diag.DK bars using green cords (#3 to 6) as KB's with blue cords (#2 and 1) as WT's. Reverse on the right half. Join blue cords at center by 2 FK's.

Series III: 4 SK's (#1 and 2); 2 SK's (#3 and 4); 2 SK's (#9 and 10); 4 SK's (#11 and 12).

Series IV: Reverse Ser. II.

Series V: Reverse Ser. I, starting with FK (#5 to 8).

Repeat designs (Ser. I to Ser. V) until the desired length is completed.

Finishing: Finish off by making Double Hor. DK bars (as at mounting end), and tying 2 blue cords into BK's.

When you wish to use a buckle for a belt instead of tying a waist band, start at the pointed end in one of the following manners (Illus. 27):

1. Mounting on a Fnd.KB by Method A (*a*).
2. Mounting on a Fnd.KB by Method B (*b*).
3. Mounting FK's, and adding on a loop at a time to make FK's into a pointed shape (*c*).

Illus. 26. Almost any kind of cords or yarns make charming bands. There is no limit to the designs one can create to make them. Instead of jewelry, wear a hand-knotted neckpiece for decoration. (See page 25.)

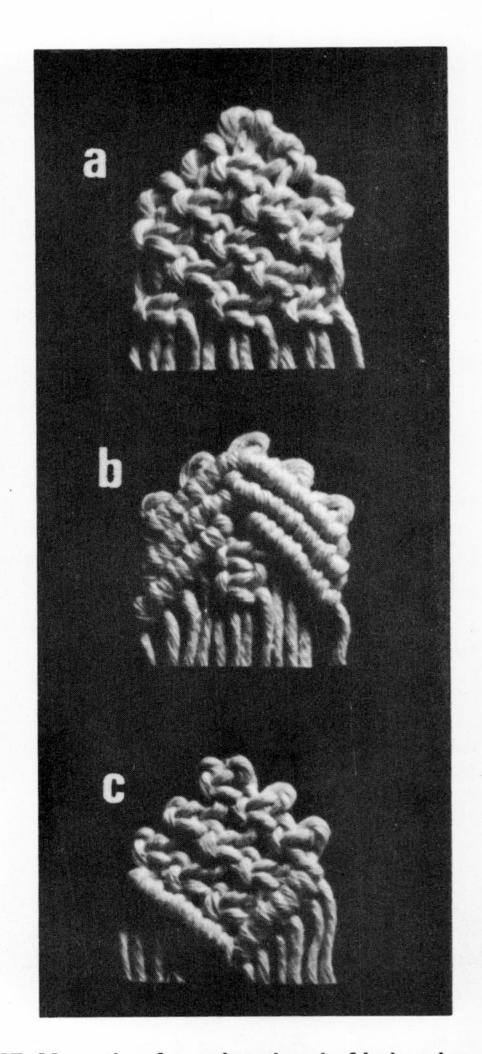

Illus. 27. Mounting for pointed end of belt using: a: Method A. b: Method B. c: FK's.

Fill in center part with FK's or the design you intend to use. At the other end of the belt, fold over the buckle bar, then sew a piece of fabric over the cord ends or simply insert them through the loops on the underside. Secure further by SK's.

Designs used on the bands may be used as

Illus. 28. This piece might be attractive as fringe for a rug, and the wool rug yarn used here would be practical. This design, which looks quite intricate, is made of a combination of the basic knots.

repeat motifs joining groups accordingly, for making fringes, bags or any other piece, following general instructions for each article.

Green-Pink Fringe in Illus. 28

Recommended material: Heavy rug yarns.

Length of strands: Pink: 28 inches (doubled); green: 26 inches (doubled).

Mounting: Mount 8 loops by Method B using 8 BK's instead of picots, in the order of: 1 pink, 6 green, 1 pink BK's, to make a group of 16 cords (#1 to 16) for each design, to be repeated across work.

Make a second Hor.DK bar across using a new strand for KB.

Design: Series I: 5 Half SK's (#1 and 2) sinnet. 5 Half FK's (#3 to 6) sinnet. Repeat across row, ending with 5 Half SK's (#15 and 16) sinnet of the last group.

Series II: Take another strand as KB and make a third Hor.DK bar across.

Series III: 2 SK's (#1 and 2). 2 FK's (#7 to 10), 2 FK's (#15 and 16 with #1 and 2 of next group), repeat across, ending with 2 SK's (#15 and 16) of last group.

Series IV: Closed Double R Diag.DK bar,

starting with #3 as KB and #4 to 8 as WT's. Reverse on the right half. Join KB's by SK.

Series V: Open L Diag.DK bars, using #3 to 8 as KB's with #2 and 1 as WT's. Reverse on the right half.

Series VI: R Diag.DK bar, using #1 as KB with #2 to 6 as WT's. Reverse on the right half.

Series VII: Pink cords: 6 FK's (#7 to 10) sinnet.

Series VIII: Green cords: make three chains: 18 Single BHK's (#1 and 2), 13 Single BHK's (#3 and 4), 9 Single BHK's (#5 and 6). Reverse on the right half.

Series IX: FK (#5 and 12 as WT's); CFK (#3 and 14 as WT's); CFK (#1 and 16 as WT's).

Finishing: Gather all cords together with pink ones on top and make a tassel with 2 CK's. Cut cord ends evenly to desired length.

Blue-Green-Yellow Fringe in Illus. 29

Recommended material: Heavy rug yarns.

Length of strands: 22 inches (doubled) for each color.

Mounting: Mount 8 loops by Method B, in the order of: 2 green, 1 yellow, 2 blue, 1 yellow, 2 green, to make 16 cords (#1 to 16) for each design, to be repeated across the work.

Design: Series I: SK (#1 and 2). FK (#7 to 10); FK (#15 and 16 with #1 and 2 of next group) across row, ending with SK #15 and 16 of last group.

Series II: Open R Diag.DK bars, using #1 to 4 as KB's with #5 to 8 as WT's. Reverse on right half.

Series III: Make a sinnet of 3 SK's (#1 and 2). CFK at center (green) using double strands (#5 and 6 with #11 and 12 as WT's). Make a petal design using #15 and 16 with #1 and 2 of next group, in the same manner as the inner petal of the gold band in Illus. 26*e* was made.

Repeat across, ending with a sinnet of 3 SK's (#15 and 16) of last group.

Series IV: Reverse Ser. II.

Series V: FK (#7 to 10). Open Double R Diag. DK bars, using #6 and 5 as KB's, with #7 and 8 as WT's. Reverse on the right half. Make a tassel of 4 yellow cords with 2 CK's and cut to desired length.

Series VI: Closed 4 L Diag.DK bars, starting with #4 as KB and #3, 2 and 1 as WT's; Open Double Vertical DK bars, using #6 and 7 as KB's with #4 to 1 as WT's. Reverse on the right half.

Finishing: Gather all green and blue cords together and make a tassel with 2 CK's. Cut cord ends evenly to the desired length.

Brown-Red Fringe in Illus. 30

Recommended material: Heavy rug yarns.

Length of strands: 45 inches (doubled) for brown and 50 inches for red.

Mounting: Mount 8 loops in the order of: 2 red, 4 brown, 2 red, to make 16 cords (#1 to 16) for each design to be repeated across the work. Mount by Method B, using 2 FK's instead of picots.

Design: Series I: FK (#1 to 4); SK (#8 and 9); FK (#13 to 16).

Series II: First group of red cords: Open L Diag. DK bars, using #2, 3 and 4 as KB's with #1 as

WT, then finish the ends of the bars as Closed Diag. DK bars. FK (#1 to 4).

Second group of red cords: Open 4 L Diag. DK bars, using #1 to 4 of next group as KB's with #16 to 13 as WT's; FK (#13 to 16); FK (#1 to 4 of next group), repeat across row, ending the same way as the first group of red cords.

Series III: Brown cords: Closed Double L Diag. DK bars, starting with #4 as KB and #3, 2 and 1 as WT's. Reverse on the right half.

Series IV: Reverse Ser. III. Join KB's by SK.

Series V: L Diag.DK using #5 to 8 with #4 as WT; Open R Diag.DK bars, using #3 and 2 as KB's with #5 to 8 as WT's; L Diag.DK bars using #5 to 8 as KB's with #1 as WT. Reverse on the right half. FK (#5 to 8); FK (#9 to 12).

Series VI: Start row with right half of Ser. III and Ser. IV, then Ser. II (as second group of red cords), then left half of Ser. III and Ser. IV.

Series VII: Reverse Ser. V.

Repeat Ser. I to Ser. V.

Finishing: 2 FK's (#7 to 10). Closed Double R Diag.DK bars, starting with #1 as KB and #2 to 8 as WT's. Reverse on the right half.

Gather cords of the same colors together with 2 CK's to form tassels. Cut tassels to desired length.

Handbags

There are different ways of starting a bag. You may use a ready-made bag handle which comes in many different styles. If the handle is equipped with a bar, this is used as the Fnd.KB on which to mount the loops. Some bag handles are styled for sewing on. The macramé work can thus be sewn on after it has been completed.

A band or drawstring may also serve as a handle for a bag, using any of the designs for bands in this book or just a simple three-strand braid.

Bags may be worked out in two separate sides (front and back) and then seamed together at both left and right sides with a needle and thread or the same cord or yarn used in the macramé work. Or, you may work the bag in one continuous circular piece.

The beauty of the designs is enhanced by lining the bag with a suitable fabric of the same or a contrasting color, whichever you prefer. The bottom side may be joined together in tassels or by SK's on the inner side of the bag.

Here are two examples of bag styles which seem to be quite popular, especially with the younger set. The off-white and gold bag shown in Illus. 32 was made from heavy packaging cord and rug yarn. It may be made larger by increasing the number of strands and the number or rows of designs.

Illus. 29. Cotton rug yarns were used in this fringe. The design is made of Diagonal DK bars. (See page 30.)

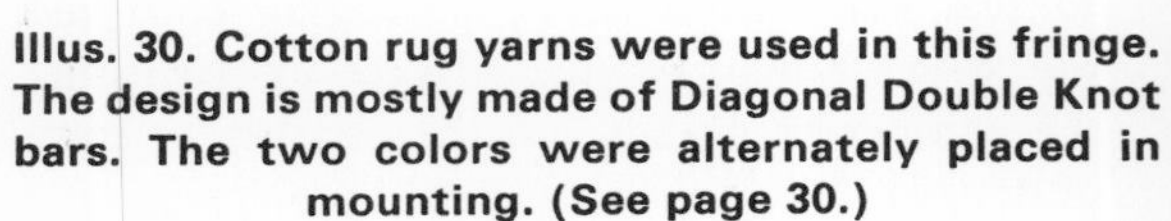

Illus. 30. Cotton rug yarns were used in this fringe. The design is mostly made of Diagonal Double Knot bars. The two colors were alternately placed in mounting. (See page 30.)

Illus. 31. Off-white and gold bag (made with off-white heavy cotton cord and gold rug yarn).

Off-White and Gold Bag in Illus. 31

Length of strands: 4 times (doubled) the length of the finished bag.

Mounting: This bag is worked in one continuous circular piece. Mount loops by *Method C* (directions for this mounting appear below), using 2 FK's for the first row and 4 FK's for the second row instead of Single FK's.

For mounting Method C (Illus. 32), make two separate Single FK's and fasten each to the WB, side by side. Then take two cords from the first FK (#3 and 4) and two cords from the second FK (#1 and 2) and make another FK (second row).

Illus. 32. Mounting by Method C.

Continue to add on Single FK's in the same manner, joining the second to the third FK, and so on. Multiple FK's may be used instead of Singles.

Make a third row of 2 FK's, joining sinnets of FK's in the same manner.

Design: The design is composed of 8 cords (#1 to 8) to be repeated across the row, starting from the third cord (#3) of the preceding FK:

Series I: Closed Double L Diag.DK bars, starting with #4 as KB and #3, 2 and 1 as WT's. Reverse on the right half. Repeat across row, joining KB's by SK.

Start about ½ inch away from preceding bars:

Series II: SK (#4 and 5). Repeat Ser. I.

Repeat Ser. II once more, making 3 rows of Double DK bars.

Series III: Introduce a second color: fasten a loop (140 inches, doubled) at the left side of #1 and, using these new cords as WT's, open R Diag. DK bars with #1 to 4 as KB's. SK 2 colored cords and then reverse on the right half. SK again 2 colored cords. Repeat across row.

Series IV: Same as Ser. II. Then CFK (#2 and 7 as WT's) at center. Reverse Ser. II.

Series V: Repeat Ser. III.

Series VI: Reverse Ser. II twice.

Finishing: Take a new strand for KB, about 22 inches long, and make a Hor.DK bar across using each of the cords as WT's. Take 2 strands from the front side and 2 opposite strands from the back side of the bag and tie into SK, then form a tassel with 2 CK's. Repeat across the bottom of bag. Cut cord ends evenly to the desired length. Insert a drawstring braid through the second row of the mounting line. Sew a suitable fabric lining on the inner side of the bag.

Red-Green Bag in Illus. 33 *(front cover)*

Recommended material: Heavy rug yarns or dyed cotton cords.

Length of strands: 5 times (doubled) for green, and 5½ times (doubled) for red, the length of the finished bag.

Mounting: For the front side of bag: using Method A, mount 10 loops of red and 20 loops of green strands in the order of: 1 red, 4 green, 1 red for each group. To make a wider bag, add multiples of 12 cords of the same color proportions, and for a longer bag, repeat any row.

There are five rows of different designs, each repeated across the work.

Take a strand, about 12 inches long, as KB, and make a Hor.DK bar with each of the cords across as WT's.

Designs: Row I: 4 SK's sinnet (first red cords). 4 FK's sinnets across row, ending with 4 SK's sinnet (last red cords).

Make a second Hor.DK bar as above.

Row II: Series I: Green cords (#1 to 8): Closed Double L Diag.DK bars, starting with #4 as KB and #3, 2 and 1 as WT's. Reverse on the right half.

Series II: CK (#1 as WT with the first two red cords). FK (#3 to 6) at center; CFK (#8 and 1) of next group, with red cords in-between. Repeat across row, ending with CK (#8 with the last two red cords).

Series III: Reverse Close Double Diag. bars in Ser. I.

Make a third Hor.DK bar.

Row III: Design is composed of 12 cords (#1 to 12): 2 red, 8 green, 2 red.

Series I: 2 FK's (#5 to 8).

Series II: Open L Diag.DK bars using #3 to 6 as KB's with #2 and 1 as WT's. Reverse on the right half.

Series III: FK (#1 to 4). FK (#5 to 8); CFK at center using double strands #9 and 10 with #3 and 4 of next group; repeat across row, ending with FK (#9 to 12 of last group).

Series IV: Reverse Ser. II and Ser. I.

Make a fourth Hor.DK bar.

Row IV: Red cords: 12 Half SK's sinnet, using the first two red cords. 12 Half FK's sinnet, using the other groups of red cords, across row, ending with 12 Half SK's sinnet, using the last two red cords.

Green cords: Series I: Closed Double R Diag. DK bars, starting with #1 as KB and #2, 3 and 4 as WT's. Reverse on the right half.

Join red cord on the left with #1 by SK; red cord on the right with #8 by SK. FK (#3 to 6) at center, and repeat as for red and for green cords as above.

Make a fifth Hor.DK bar.

Row V: Series I: Same as Row III, Ser. I and Ser. II.

Series II: Same as Row I.

Finishing: Finish off with triple Hor.DK bars, using three different KB's.

The back side of this bag may be knotted using the same designs as the front side. When completed, put two faces together and tie opposite KB's along the left and right sides and opposite cords at the bottom by SK's. Then turn to face out. Make a band using any design or just a thick braid to the desired length. Make a BK near each end for tassels. Sew over the seams along the left and right sides of bag. Line bag with a suitable fabric.

You may choose to make the back side of the bag with a simpler design. Here is your chance to create your own. Using the same number of rows as on the front side, make something like the FK's in Illus. 16.

Flaps for bags may be made in the same manner as for the pointed end of the belt. (For mounting, see Illus. 27.) When fringes on these flaps are preferred, mount by Method B. Use longer picots (about 3 to 4 inches), then cut into fringes.

Miscellaneous Projects

Yellow Neckpiece in Illus. 34b

Recommended material: Mercerized cotton, nylon or metallic cords about 1/16 inch or 1 mm. thickness.

Length of strands: Make a band using Half FK's sinnet to the desired length (to go around the neck). Allow longer outer cords (#1 and 4), about 7 times the length of the inner cords.

Mounting: Use a curtain ring (1½ inches diameter) for Fnd.KB. Measure and cut 32 strands, 12 inches (doubled) each. Mount by Method A. Cover the exposed part of the ring with Double BHK's.

Design is composed of 10 cords (#1 to 10), repeated 8 times.

Series I: Closed Triple R Diag.DK bars, starting with #1 as KB and #2 to 5 as WT's. Reverse on the right half. Join KB's by SK. Join last cord of one group to the first cord of the next group by SK.

Finishing: Finish off with 2 CFK's using double strands (#1 and 2 with #9 and 10 as WT's). Then make 2 CK's to form tassels. Do not cut cord ends, to simulate a sunburst.

a b

Illus. 34. These two neckpieces were made with mercerized cotton cord. They would look striking on a dark piece of clothing.

Place Mat (12 inches by 16 inches) in Illus. 35

Recommended material: Dyed cotton or sisal cords, ($\frac{1}{10}$ inch thickness).

Length of strands: $4\frac{1}{2}$ times (doubled) the length of the finished mat.

Mounting: Mount 30 loops by Method A.

Design is composed of 12 cords (#1 to 12) and is repeated across row. Start about 1 inch away from the mounting line.

Row I: Make diamond motifs with a "bud" at center:

Series I: SK (#6 and 7). Closed Double L Diag. DK bars, starting with #6 as KB and #5 to 1 as WT's. Reverse on the right half. Join KB's between groups by SK.

Make a "bud" at center, about $\frac{1}{4}$ inch from the

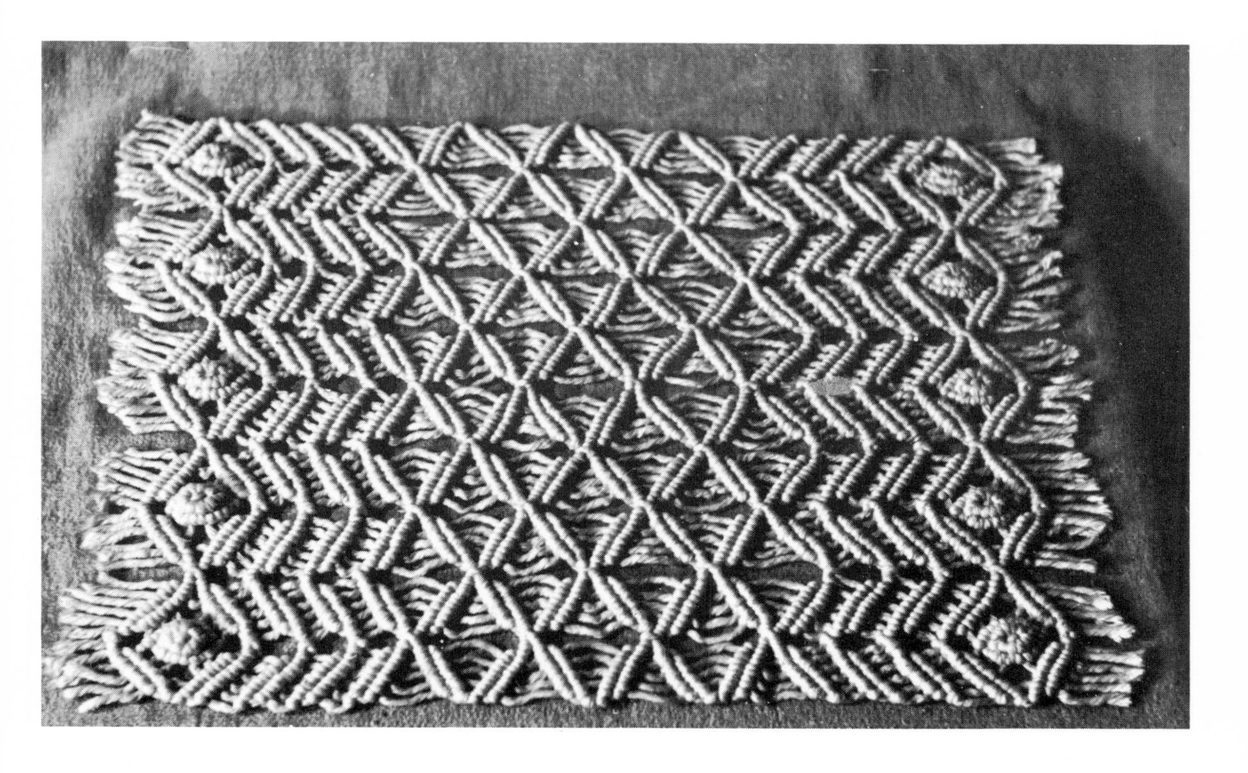

Illus. 35. Place mat.

Illus. 36. Inserting cord end on the underside of preceding DK's.

bars. (Directions for making the "bud" are on page 26 under Gold Band in Illus 26*e*.)

Series II: Reverse Ser. I

Row II to Row IV: Same as Row I Ser. II (omit "bud").

Row V: Same as Row I Ser. I.

Row VI: Same as Row I Ser. II.

Row VII: Same as Row I Ser. I.

At this point, you have completed the first half of the place mat. Now, reverse on the other half; that is, Row VII back to Row I. Trim cord ends to about 1 inch. Pull out the Fnd.KB at the mounting line and trim in the same way.

If fringes are not desired, you may start mounting by Method B and make 2 additional successive Hor.DK bars, finishing off with 3 successive Hor. DK bars. Turn work to underside and, with the aid of a crochet hook, insert each cord end through the loop of the preceding DK, as in Illus. 36. Trim off ends and secure further by applying waterproof glue or cement.

Shaping

When shapes are made of big curves as in the wall hanging in Illus. 37, you may place a sheet of paper on which the pattern is drawn between the working surface and your macramé work, as a guide. See Illus. 38. This method is also applicable for irregular outlines, such as for making blouses or other parts of garments.

Circular Work

For lamp shades, bags, cylindrical hangings, etc., any mounting method may be used. When mounting by Methods A and B, the Fnd.KB is tied together at the ends to form a circle or ring. Then work in a circular direction. The diameter may be varied by using a shorter or longer Fnd. KB. Method C was used for the bag in Illus. 31.

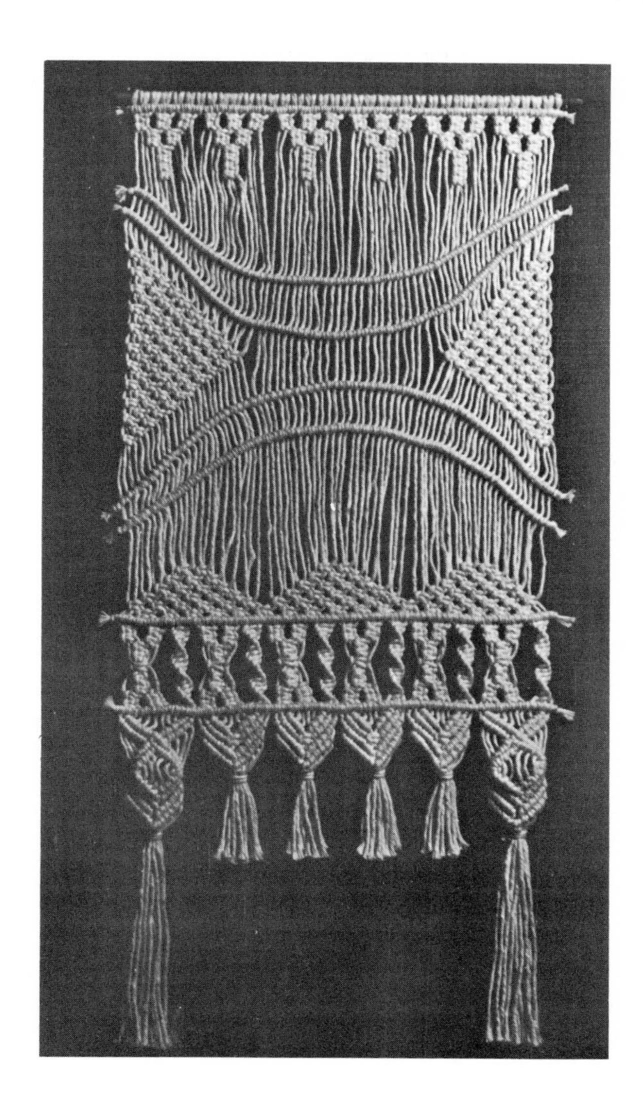

Illus. 37. Heavy cotton cord was used in this wall hanging. This design can easily be adapted to a window shade, using a much heavier cord. Curtain rod may be used for Foundation Knot Bearer (Fnd.KB).

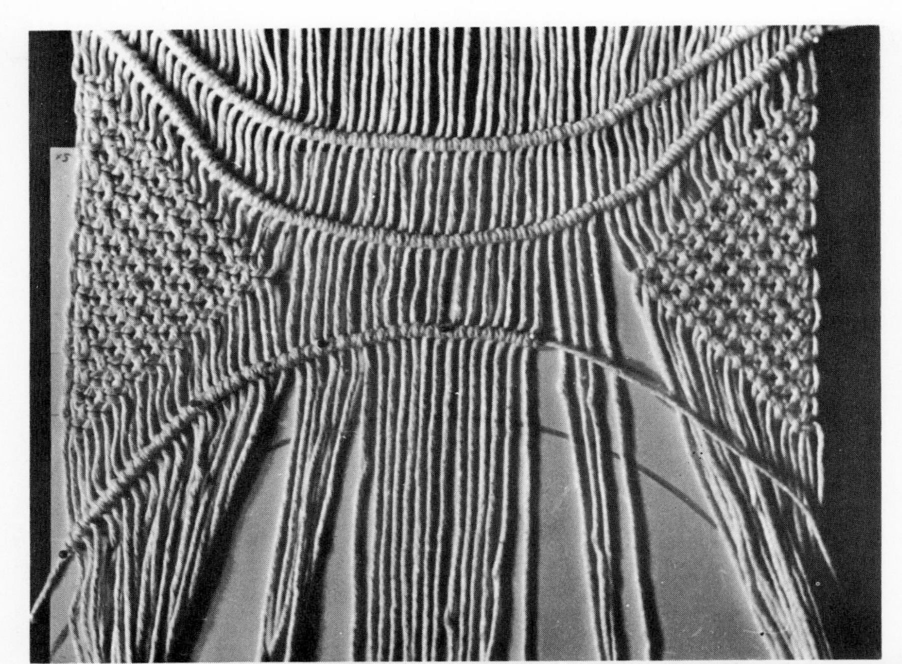

Illus. 38. Pattern drawn on a sheet of paper is used as a guide for the curved DK bars.

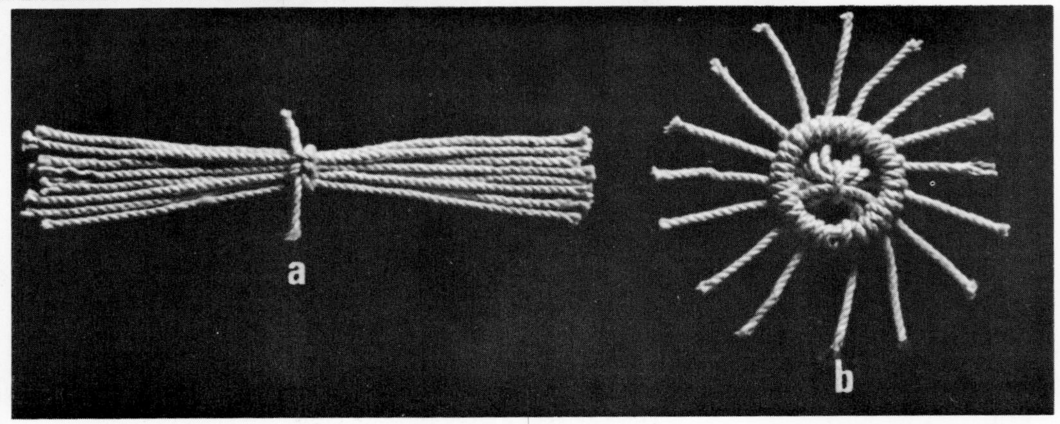

Illus. 40. a: Loop was added on. b: FK was added on.

Another method of mounting that you may use is *Method D*: using a piece of cord first tie the required number of loops together by a SK; fasten with a pin onto the WB, with the SK face down. Take another piece of cord about 10 inches long and, using this as KB, make a circular DK bar about $\frac{1}{2}$ to 1 inch away from the center. Join ends of the KB by SK, and then proceed to knot the design. See Illus. 39.

Illus. 41. This flat circular piece was made by mounting according to Method A, and then making a second row of DK bars. New cords were added as the work progressed by simply inserting loops or Flat Knots between groups of threads.

Illus. 39 (left). Mounting for circular work—Method D. a: The loops are tied together by SK. b: Circular DK bar is made.

When making a flat round piece, such as a doily or round pillow-top, you will need to add new cords as you go. This may be done by simply pinning down a new loop or a new FK between groups of cords as needed. Then continue to work out the design. (Illus. 40). In the doily in Illus. 41, new loops and FK's were added in every row.

Tassels

Decorative Tassels are used as pulls or ends of a narrow band. Here is another chance for you to create your own designs. Use 10 or 12 filler strands to make a fuller tassel and 8 or 12 WT's. Length of WT's should be at least $1\frac{1}{2}$ times (double) the filler strands. Use multiples of 4, 6 or 8 cords depending on the design you choose. Tie loops together (Illus. 42*a*) as in Method D, using a piece of cord long enough for the intended use. (This may be knotted into a band or twisted into a cord.) Let the WT's lie on top. Fold all cords down and temporarily tie the filler cords together (Illus. 42*b*), so that they don't get into the knotting itself. Take another piece of cord and wind three times around all the strands, joining the ends by SK to make a head. Then proceed to work the design around. You may finish off with a Hor. DK bar before trimming the cord ends evenly.

Illus. 42. How to make a decorative tassel.

When creating your own projects, it is wise to first sketch a plan of the finished shape and designs to be used before actually starting to knot. Whether you follow the directions in this book or decide to create your own, you will find that macramé is indeed a very enjoyable and fascinating art. Every piece you make will bring you the great pleasure of being a creative artist.

Illus. 43. Christmas hanging with "capiz" shells. It was made with white heavy cotton cord.

Illus. 44. Wall hanging made with heavy wool rug yarn. Wood dowel is the Fnd.KB.

Illus. 45. The designs on these tassels are made of one or a combination of Flat Knots and Double Knots.

Illus. 46. This wall hanging is made of weaving yarns. Flat Knots were used on the side portions, and Double Bar Knots on the red and blue panel.

Illus. 47. Heavy India packaging cord was used for this piece. There is no definite design here, showing the great freedom one has, using only a few basic knots. The thread ends were neatly tucked under on the sides.

Illus. 48. Bodice of an evening dress, worn over black leotards. It was made with white cotton cord.

Abbreviations

BHK	Button Hole Knot
BK	Bead Knot
CK	Collecting Knot
CFK	Collecting Flat Knot
DK	Double Knot
FK	Flat Knot
Fnd.KB	Foundation Knot Bearer
Hor.	Horizontal
KB	Knot Bearer
L Diag.	Left Diagonal
R Diag.	Right Diagonal
Ser.	Series
Sub-Ser.	Sub-Series
SK	Simple or Square Knot
WB	Working Base
WT	Working Thread

Index